HYDROPONIC SYSTEM

Winter, summer, every season.
Complete beginner's guide; learn to grow
fruits, vegetables, herbs without a garden.
Inexpensive, sustainable and complete.

Don't spend a fortune, diy

THEODORE MONCANTO

This document is geared towards providing exact and reliable information with regard to the topic and issue covered. The publication is sold with the idea that the publisher is not required to render accounting, officially permitted or otherwise qualified services. If advice is necessary, legal or professional, a practiced individual in the profession should be ordered.

From a Declaration of Principles which was accepted and approved equally by a Committee of the American Bar Association and a Committee of Publishers and Associations:

The information provided herein is stated to be truthful and consistent, in that any liability, in terms of inattention or otherwise, by any usage or abuse of any policies, processes, or directions contained within is the solitary and utter responsibility of the recipient reader. Under no circumstances will any legal responsibility or blame be held against the publisher for any reparation, damages, or monetary loss due to the information herein, either directly or indirectly.

The information herein is offered for informational purposes solely and is universal as so. The presentation of the information is without contract or any type of guarantee assurance.

The trademarks that are used are without any consent, and the publication of the trademark is without permission or backing by the trademark owner. All trademarks and brands within this book are for clarifying purposes only and are owned by the owners themselves, not affiliated with this document.

DISCLAIMER

By accessing this eBook, you accept this disclaimer in full.

No part of this eBook may be reproduced or transmitted in any form or by any means, electronic or mechanical, without written permission from the author.

The information provided within this eBook is for general informational purposes only. Even though we have attempted to present accurate information, there are no representations or warranties, express or implied, about the completeness, accuracy, or reliability of the information, products, services, or related graphics contained in this eBook for any purpose. The information is provided "as is," to be used at your own risk.

The methods described in this eBook represent the author's personal experiences. They are not intended to be a definitive set of instructions for this project. You may discover there are other methods and materials to accomplish the same end result. Your results may differ.

This eBook includes information regarding the products and services by third parties. We do not assume responsibility for any third party materials or opinions. Use of recommended third party materials does not guarantee that your results will mirror third party results or our own. Publication of such third party material is just a recommendation and expression of the authors' personal opinions. Any reliance on the third party material is at your own risk.

All trademarks appearing in this eBook are the property of their respective owners.

No warranty may be created or extended by any promotional statements for this work. The author shall not be liable for any damages arising herefrom.

TABLE OF CONTENTS

INTRODUCTION

Hydroponics is a kind of soilless cultivation in which plants are grown in nutrient solutions, with or without an artificial medium. Hydroponics is highly productive; it is a device that protects water and the land. It is ecologically sound too. Hydroponics gardening is high-tech but requires only basic farming skills to get started. It is important to control the air and root temperatures including factors such as light, water, plant nutrition and extreme climates. For this reason hydroponic systems must also work in temperature-controlled environments such as greenhouses. It is very important to pay close attention to the conditions of the greenhouse, otherwise hydroponics will stop being cost-effective for you.

For liquid hydroponic systems there is no carrying media for the plant roots. This is also known as solution culture; the three main types of solution culture are the solution culture, the continuous flow solution culture, and aeroponics.

For the former, plants are cultivated for containers with hydroponic nutrient solution. These are typically applications at home where hydroponic systems operate in glass bottles, plastic pots, tubs, and tanks. The solution is always gently aerated but can also be unaerated, in which case the solution amount is small enough to allow access to the regular supply of oxygen to the roots. The nutrient solution, normally once a week, is revised according to a set timetable.

Continuous flux solution activity is formulated differently, with the hydroponic solution flowing past the surface. A common variant of this culture is the nutrient film technique; here, a very shallow stream of water, containing all the dissolved nutrients required for plant growth, is circulated past plant roots. The hydroponic nutrient solution flows in the lower half of the roots, creating a watertight root layer whereas the upper parts of the roots are exposed to air and obtain good oxygen supply.

Aggregate hydroponic systems however also provide a source of solid natural or artificial support. Could there be hydroponic systems, too? Where the nutrient solution is dispersed and not reused or capped to the plant roots, where the excess solution can be recovered, replenished, and recycled.

-- crop has very different requirements and hydroponics have to pay attention to the unique needs of each crop, as they do in any form of farming. Today, hydroponic systems are growing rapidly, and yields are consistently numerous, hitting heights that we have never foreseen. Hydroponics is feasible in areas such as deserts, and space stations where there is no natural farming. People living in heavily populated areas may use hydroponics to grow their own fresh vegetables in windows or rooftop gardens. Hydroponically grown plants also grow faster, and are relatively free from soil-borne diseases.

If you are interested in gardening which can be simple and quiet and you want to grow your own plants, the hydroponics gardening cycle will help you grow your own plants without effort. Hydroponic gardening helps produce large and tasty vegetables and fruits. Personal hydroponics garden can be built anywhere around you. It's not very difficult and attention-attracting method of gardening compared to traditional pot growing. It's the soilless method of rising. Hydroponics, also known as aquatic farming, involves nutrient-containing water in agriculture.

Ideally, soil acts as a nutrient reservoir but soil is not required for plant production. Plants dissolved in water will consume the plants needing essential nutrients to grow, and soil is not required if these nutrients are supplied artificially.

The water supply in hydroponics gardening can be automated and recycled, this reduces water costs. Hydroponics system needs no compost, soil is not a essential hydroponic gardening medium. Within the hydroponics system important macro- and micronutrients are pumped through inert medium for advantageous hydroponic yields. Hydroponic systems may be carefully supervised when installed in a greenhouse or other controlled ambience. Hydroponics is mostly a science but it is often done as a hobby. Hydroponics allows planting in regions where traditional planting is impossible.

In modern gardening, plagues like, pin worms, white flies, leaf miners, nematodes and diseases like root rot and bacterial wilt kill plants. Hydroponics system helps reduce the risk of disease and pests caused by drained water sterilization, and hydroponic plants are given regular heat treatment and ultraviolet radiation. Growing plants are useless when plants are destroyed by pests and diseases at the later stage of growth; hence, hydroponics is a common technique for producing larger, more pest-free and delicious hydroponic fruits and vegetables. For an effective management plan for hydroponics one should identify potential crop disease and insect problem, and then use the available solution to eliminate disease and insect problem.

Hydroponics will assist in the effective resolution of unexpected food shortages. Hydroponics is the future of mass cultivation; contamination of the groundwater is minimized, and no drainage system is required. You will have complete control over your plant production with the aid of the hydroponics.

CHAPTER ONE

History of Hydroponics

The first known work on soilless grown terrestrial plants was the 1627 book Sylva Sylvarum or Francis Bacon's 'A Natural History,' written one year after his death. After that, water culture became a common investigation technique. John Woodward published his studies on spearmint water culture in 1699. He has found plants growing faster in less-pure water sources than plants in purified water. By 1842, a list of nine elements considered important to plant growth had been compiled, and the findings of German botanists Julius von Sachs and Wilhelm Knop in the years 1859–75 contributed to the invention of the soilless cultivation technique. Development of soilless terrestrial plants in solutions to mineral nutrients has been called culture of solution. It soon became a common technique for study and teaching, and is still commonly used. Solution culture is, now called, a kind of hydroponics where an inert medium is present.

Some plant diseases were investigated by plant scientists around the 1930s, and symptoms related to existing soil conditions were observed. Water culture studies have been conducted in this context in the goal of producing specific symptoms under controlled conditions. In 1929, the University of California at Berkeley's William Frederick Gericke (August 30, 1882-September 29, 1970) began actively advocating the use of solution culture for agricultural crop production. He first named it aquaculture but later found aquaculture already being applied to aquatic organism culture. Gericke created a sensation in his backyard by growing tomato vines twenty-five feet (7.6 meters) high in mineral nutrient solutions rather than soil. In 1937, he coined the word hydroponics, water culture, suggested to him by W. A. Setchell, a psychologist with an comprehensive classical education.

Unfortunately Gericke overlooked that the time for the general scientific application of hydroponics was not yet ready. Reports of Gericke's research and his predictions that plant agriculture would revolutionize hydroponics prompted a large number of requests for more information. Because of the administration's distrust, Gericke had been refused the use of the University's greenhouses for his studies, so when the University attempted to pressure him to disclose his home-developed preliminary nutrient recipes, he asked for greenhouse space and time to refine them using correct testing facility. Although he was ultimately given greenhouse space, Hoagland and Arnon were assigned by the University to re-evaluate Gericke 's claims and prove his theory had little advantage over the yields of soil grown plants, a view held by Hoagland. In 1940, after leaving his academic position in 1937 in a environment that was politically unfavorable, Gericke published the novel, Complete Guide to Soilless Gardening Therein, for the first time, he published his simple formula for hydroponically grown plants that included the macro- and micronutrient salts.

Dennis Robert Hoagland and Daniel Israel Arnon wrote a classic 1938 agricultural bulletin, The Water Culture Method for Growing Plants Without Soil, which stated that hydroponic crop yields were no better than crop yields with good-quality soils, as a result of research on Gericke's claims by the University of California. In the end, crop yields would be limited by factors other than mineral nutrients, particularly light ones. Nevertheless, this research did not fully consider the other main advantages of hydroponics, including the fact that the plant's roots have continuous access to oxygen and that the plants have access to as much or as little water as they need. It is vital as one of the most common mistakes when growing is overwatering and underwatering; and hydroponics prevents this from happening because vast quantities of water can be made available to the plant, which can overwhelm root systems in the soil, and any excess water is drained away, recirculated or effectively aerated, thus preventing anoxic conditions. A grower has to be very knowledgeable in soil to know exactly how much water the plant requires to eat. Too much and the plant will not be able to access oxygen; too little, and the plant will lose the ability to bring nutrients that are normally transferred through the roots when in solution. The views of Hoagland and the University's helpful support led these two researchers to create a variety of new formulas for mineral nutrient solutions, commonly known as Hoagland solution. Modified Hoagland solutions will continue to be employed, as will Gericke 's proposed hydroponic techniques.

Some of the first hydroponics achievements occurred on Wake Island, a rocky atoll in the Pacific Ocean used by Pan American Airlines as a refueling stop. Throughout the 1930s Hydroponics was used there to cultivate passenger vegetables. Hydroponics was a must on Wake Island, because there was no soil, and airlifting in fresh vegetables was prohibitively expensive[22].

From 1943 to 1946, Daniel I. Arnon served as a major in the U.S. Army and used his previous plant nutrition experience to feed troops stationed on the barren Ponape Island in the western Pacific by growing crops in gravel and nutrient-rich water, as no arable land was available.

Nutrient film technique was invented by Allen Cooper of England in the 1960s. The Land Pavilion at Walt Disney World's EPCOT Center opened in 1982 and incorporates a range of hydroponic techniques in prominence.

For its Managed Ecological Life Support System (CELSS) NASA has carried out extensive hydroponic work in recent decades. Hydroponics work imitating a Martian setting uses LED light to expand with far less heat in a broad range of colours. Ray Wheeler, a plant physiologist at the Space Life Science Lab at Kennedy Space Center, suggests that as a bioregenerative life support device, hydroponics can produce advancements in space travel.

In 2007 Eurofresh Farms sold over 200 million pounds of hydroponically grown tomatoes in Willcox, Arizona. Eurofresh has 318 acres (1.3 km2) under glass and represents about a third of the U.S. commercial greenhouse hydroponic sector. Eurofresh tomatoes were pesticide-free and grown in highly irrigated rockwool. Eurofresh had declared bankruptcy, and NatureSweet Ltd. purchased the greenhouses in 2013.

Canada had hundreds of acres of large commercial hydroponic greenhouses as of 2017, producing tomatoes, peppers, and cucumbers.

The global hydroponics market is expected to rise from US$ 226.45 million in 2016 to US$ 724.87 million by

2023, owing to technical developments within the industry and various economic factors.

CHAPTER TWO

Techniques of Hydroponic Growing

True hydroponics is plant growth without a rooting medium, in a nutrient solution. Plant roots are either suspended in a standing aerated nutrient solution or in a nutrient solution that flows through a root tube, or plant roots are sprinkled with a nutrient solution regularly. This description is somewhat different from the widely accepted hydroponics term, which in the past included all types of hydroponic / soilless production. Those three hydroponic growing techniques will be addressed in the first section of this chapter. Hydroponic systems using inorganic rooting media will be discussed in the second portion.

Mediumless Hydroponic Systems

Standing Aerated Nutrient Solution

This is the oldest hydroponic technique, dating back to those early investigators who used this process in the mid-1800s to determine the elements were important for plants. In the 1840s Sachs and the other early investigators grew plants in aerated solutions and observed the effect of adding different substances to the nutrient solution on plant growth (Russell, 1950). This technique is still of use for different types of plant nutrition studies, although some researchers have turned to nutrient solution flowing and continuous replenishment procedures.

The requirements regarding the technique of aerated standing nutrient solution are:

1. A fitting rooting vessel
2. A gateway to nutrients
3. An air tube and pump to continuously bubble up air into the nutrient solution.

The bubbling air helps both to add and inject O2 to the nutrient solution. The widely used formula is Hoagland's or some version of it as developed by Berry (1985), with the plant nutrient solution volume ratio of 1 plant per 2 to 4 gallons of nutrient solution (9 to 18 litres).

The nutrient solution may need periodic replacement, usually every 5 to 10 days, frequency dependent on plant number and size, as well as nutrient solution volume. Water loss from the nutrient solution would need to be replaced daily, either using nutrient-free water (pure water) or a diluted (1/10th strength) nutrient solution, as there is a danger that any additional nutrient elements that alter the initial element balance and adversely affect the plants. It should also be remembered that with each day of use, root activity and element uptake will alter the pH and composition of the initial nutrient solution, changes which may have an effect on plant growth. The question becomes "is it appropriate to restore the pH and elemental content of the nutrient solution to its original levels regular before replacement? "An improvement other than water loss replacement is usually recommended in most instances.

Clark (1982) identified another aerated standing nutrient solution system; this method was used to research the basic demands of corn and sorghum. Several plants are grown in a nutrient solution of 1/2 gallon (2 L), with change periods ranging from 7 to 30 days depending on the stage of growth and plant species. In the nutrient solution, the ratio of 8 to 1 of NO3 to NH4 is used to preserve some degree of constancy in pH. While Clark's technique is specifically designed to handle nutrient solutions, it could be applied effectively to other plant species.

The hydroponic growing method of aerated standing nutrient solution has limited commercial application while lettuce and herbs were successfully grown on styrofoam sheets floating on an aerated nutrient solution. In the styrofoam the plants are put in small gaps, with their roots developing into the nutrient solution. When the plants are ready for harvest the sheets are removed from the solution.

Another reason why this hydroponic growing system is not well suited for commercial use is because water and chemical use are quite high due to the frequent replacement requirements. In addition, the nutrient solution 's composition is constantly changing, requiring monitoring and adjustment to maintain the pH and elemental ion balance and concentration levels of sufficiency over the use period, which can range from 45 to 65 days. Temperature and management of root disease are additional requirements if this growing approach is to produce positive results.

Nutrient Film Technique (NFT)

A significant development in hydroponics occurred during the 1970s with the introduction of the technique of nutrient film, often referred to as NFT (Cooper, 1976, 1979ab). Others also modified the name by using the word "flow" instead of "film" (Schippers, 1979), as the plant roots actually grow in a nutrient solution flow. When Allen Cooper first presented his hydroponic growing system NFT (1976), it was heralded as the future hydroponic process. Indeed it was the first significant improvement in the technique of hydroponic development since the 1930s. At the conference entitled "Hydroponics Worldwide: State of the Art in Soilless Crop Growth" (Savage, 1985a), Cooper and his colleagues addressed their experiences with this process, which left those present with the impression that hydroponics research had taken a significant step forward.

However, experience has shown that the NFT approach does not solve the may problems that most hydroponic growing systems inherit. How-ever in many parts of the world, especially in Western Europe and England, this has not deterred its rapid acceptance and usage. NFT has been extensively debated and tested (Khudheir and Newton, 1983; Hurd, 1985; Cooper, 1985, 1988; Edwards, 1985; Gerber, 1986; Molyneux, 1988; Hochmuth, 1991b), but its potential remains highly uncertain unless there are effective ways to manage the disease and nutrient solutions. Cooper (1985) proposed a shift in the nature of the trough, from the "U" shape to a "W" (called a divided gully system), in which the plant base sets at the top of the W center with the roots separated on either side of the W. To keep the roots moist with nutrient solution, a capillary mate is placed on the inverted "V" portion of the "W" This redesign of the single-gully NFT system, as initially suggested by Cooper (1976, 1979ab), has a range of advantages. A portion of the plant roots — that on the inverted "V" — is in air; a portion of the roots lies on a moist surface (capillary matting), which allows for better oxygenation of the rooting system; and the remaining root mass is now split into two channels, which would mitigate the problems associated with a large mass of roots in one channel. It is now possible to use two different irrigation systems by flowing water, or by various types of nutrient solutions along either route. Unfortunately, design has now complicated the NFT channel system, and it is uncertain whether this change would significantly improve the performance of the plants. Cooper (1996) recently published a summary of his 1976 NFT book, in which he identified some of the problems that could occur with this technique of hydroponic development.

In the NFT system, the roots of plants are literally suspended in a trough, pipe, or gully (through is the word used from this point on) through which a nutrient solution passes. The trough containing the plant roots is placed on a slope (usually about 1 percent) to allow the nutrient solution to be applied at the top of the trough by gravity at a required flow rate of 1/4 gallon (1 L) per minute from top to bottom. The volume rate down the trough decreases as the root mat increases in size. As the nutrient solution flows down the trough, plants at the top end of the trough reduce the nutrient solution's O2 and/or elemental content, a decrease that may be sufficient to significantly affect plant growth and development at the bottom end. In fact, as the root mat becomes thicker and denser, the flowing nutrient solution continues to travel over the top and down the root mat's outer edge, reducing its interaction within the root mass. Such delay of flow results of inadequate mixing of the present flowing nutrient solution with water and the elements left behind from previous applications of nutrient solutions in the root mat. One way to mitigate these effects is to make the drill no longer than 30 feet (9 m) in length. Additionally, with longer-term crops, the trough may also be made wider, which may be more appropriate for root production.

One of NFT's major benefits is its ease of establishment and the relative low cost of construction materials. Morgan (1999c) and Smith (2004) address the nature of the NFT troughs and materials suitable for producing troughs. Simply folding a wide strip of polyethylene film into a pipe -or a triangular-like shape may form a trough. The polyethylene film can be either black or white so it must be opaque in order to keep out the light. As light reaches the trough, the growth of algae becomes a grave problem. The sheet of polyethylene is pulled around the stem of the plant, and closed with pins or clips, pipe-like rooting trough. If the trough is formed from polyethylene film strips, it can be discarded after each crop, thus requiring the permanent piping and storage tank of nutrient solution only to be sterilized.

Most troughs in use today are made of different plastic materials, with clarity, structural strength and ultraviolet (UV) resistance being the requirements. The trough size (width, height, and shape) is generally determined by the crop being cultivated. Lack of structural strength in the bottom of the trough can lead to unevenness that causes nutrient solution to lie in depressions that can lead to anaerobic conditions.

At the spacing recommended for that crop, the plants are placed in the trough. Plants are normally started in germination cubes made from fiberglass or similar material. The cube is placed directly in the trough with its plant started. Experience has shown that the cube of germination should not be made from materials which disintegrate over time. A sturdy germination cube in the NFT trough helps to hold the plant in place.

NFT systems are normally closed systems, i.e. the nutrient solution which exits the end of the trough is recovered for reuse. Bugbee (1995) addresses the management criteria of hydroponic recirculating rising systems. The introduction of maquillage water, the need to reconstitute the content of the pH and nutrient components, filtering and sterilization are procedures that must be developed. An open system would mean discarding the nutrient solution that exits the trough, which is costly in terms of water and reagent use as well as posing a problem for proper disposal (Johnson, 2002c).

If the NFT system is run as a closed system (i.e. the nutrient solution is recirculated several times until it is discarded), Cooper (1979a) has suggested the use of a special nutrient solution, called the topping-up solution, to be applied to the starting solution in order to preserve its composition during use. Normally, the nutrient solution is monitored by periodic EC measurements, which determine the appropriate times to add make-up (or topping-up) nutrient solution to maintain the initial volume and when to dump and make a new batch of nutrient solution.

Formulations of nutrient solutions suited to NFT growing systems were recommended based on conditions of crop and field management.

Aeroponics

Another promising hydroponic technique for the future was thought to be aeroponics, which is the distribution of water and essential elements by means of an aerosol mist bathing the plant roots (Nickols, 2002). One of the significant advantages of this technique compared to flowing the nutrient solution past the plant roots is aeration, as the roots are essentially growing in air. The technique was designed to achieve substantial economies in the use of both water and essential elements. The critical aspects of the technique are the character of the aerosol, frequency of root exposure, and composition of the nutrient solution. Adi Limited (1982) described an aeroponic system that it said had proven to be highly successful. The system is computer controlled and requires a special fogging device, troughs, and an array of sensing devices. Although yields of crops obtained with this growing system have been reported to be considerably above those obtained with conventional hydroponic systems, the initial cost for the Adi system plus operating costs are very high, bringing into question its commercial viability (Soffer, 1985), although its value in plant propagation is considerable (Soffer, 1988).

Several methods have employed a spray of the nutrient solution rather than a fine mist; droplet size and frequency of exposure of the roots to the nutrient solution are the critical factors. Continuous exposure of the roots to a fine mist gives better results than intermittent spraying or misting. In most aeroponic systems, a small reservoir of water is allowed to remain in the bottom of the rooting vessel so that a portion of the roots has access to a continuous supply of water. The composition of the nutrient solution would be adjusted based on the time and frequency of exposure of the roots to the nutrient solution.

Medium Hydroponic Systems

In the culture systems described in this section, plants are grown in some type of inorganic rooting medium (Straver, 1996a,b; Morgan, 2003f), with the nutrient solution applied by flooding or drip irrigation.

Ebb-and-Flow Nutrient Solution Systems

This type of hydroponic growing system has been in wide use for many years, but it is not widely used commercially today other than for growing units of the hobby / home type. The growing system consists of a watertight rooting pad, a rooting pad containing an inert rooting medium, such as gravel, coarse sand or volcanic rock, a nutrient solution sump (equal in volume to the growing bed(s)), an electrical pump to transfer the nutrient solution from the sump to the growing bed(s) and a piping system to handle the growing bed(s). The sump must be below the growing bed(s) in order to have gravity return flow of nutrient solution from the growing bed(s) into the sump. As this is a "closed" device, it will recirculate the nutrient solution until it is no longer available when it is drained and replaced with a freshly made solution. The nutrient solution should be checked for pH, EC and likely elemental content before each application, and then modified accordingly. After each circulation through the rooting bed the nutrient solution may also require filtering and sterilization.

This method of hydroponic growth was the one used by the U.S. Throughout World War II the army distributed new tomatoes and lettuce to soldiers fighting in the Pacific (Eastwood, 1947). Following WWII, this hydroponic growing technique was used by farmers in many southern states in the United States and elsewhere (Eastwood, 1947), especially tomatoes growing in outdoor hydroponic gardens. The author has advised growers who grow in both greenhouse and outdoor settings using this method.

The drawbacks of this method are root disease vulnerability, inefficient use of water and nutrient reagents, and the need for periodic replacement of the rooting medium, which is normally gravel. Throughout the 1960s and 70s an ebb-and-flow device designed to grow greenhouse tomatoes was marketed. The sump contained 2000 gallons of nutrient solution that required daily water volume adjustment as well as potential pH and nutrient item make-up changes (based on an EC measurement). Around every 2 to 3 weeks the nutrient solution required complete replacement — a considerably inefficient use of valuable water and reagents. With time, plant roots began to grow into the pipes that delivered the nutrient solution back to and from the growing bed(s) and sump, thereby limiting the flow. One diseased plant inserted into the system would result in a total crop loss. Cleanup often meant removing and replacing the rooting medium on gravel. Another problem with this system was that because they were in the ground, the sump and enclosed nutrient solution would have a temperature equal to that of the surrounding soil, meaning that the nutrient solution would be colder than the temperature of the ambient air during most of the season, an unwanted trait that would harm plants when the nutrient solution was dispensed into the growing medium.

The ebb-and-flow growing system is fairly easy to install and run on a small scale for homeowner and hobbyist, and provides reasonably good plant production with a moderate level of care.

The timing schedule for flooding the growing bed(s) will depend on the crop's atmospheric demand and growth level, as well as the growing medium's water-holding capability. Normally the nutrient solution composition is similar to, or some modification of, the basic Hoagland solution, depending on the crop and growth stage.

This hydroponic growing system has proven to be difficult to manage commercially and is very inefficient in its use of water and essential elements, important reasons for its lack of use today.

Drip/Pass-Through Inorganic Medium Systems

There are two such growing systems, one in bags, pots, or buckets, using perlite or similar inorganic rooting medium (Morgan, 2003f), and the other using rockwool slabs.

Inorganic rooting medium in sachets or pots / seals

This hydroponic growing method is commonly used today in commercial production where the plant(s) are grown in a container, bowl, or bucket of inorganic media, with perlite as the most common rooting medium (Gerhart and Gerhart, 1992; Morgan, 2003f). The bag used for transporting the perlite is laid on its side in one method, small holes are cut along the bottom edge of the bag to allow excess nutrient solution to flow out, an access hole(s) is cut in the top of the bag to position a plant, and then a drip tube is placed on the edge of the access hole next to the plant. Initially, the plant may be planted in a rockwool cube or other similar material, then placed on an opening on the container, with the drip line mounted at the plant base. In place of the shipping container, a pot or bucket, such as the BATO bucket, filled with perlite or similar inorganic material can be used. Such systems, which often use BATO buckets, are commonly used for tomato and cucumber growth.

The nutrient solution is not collected and recirculated, since this is a "safe" device. The supplied quantity should be adequate for a minor excess flow from openings cut at the bottom edge of the bag or from openings in the base of pots and buckets (the BATO bucket has a small reservoir at its base). Scheduling of the rate and timing of application of the nutrient solution depends on various factors, such as atmospheric demand, crop, and growth level. The effluent from the growing vessel may be tracked during the growing cycle for its pH and EC and changes made in the supplied nutrient solution, or the medium leached with water to extract any accumulated salts. A solution aliquot can also be drawn from the medium itself shortly after irrigation to perform the same measurements as made on an effluent sample.

The perlite-containing vessel may be used or discarded one more time at the end of the growing season, making the system relatively easy to install and replace at reasonable cost. Specific modifications have been made to this growing device to accommodate various crop types. One example is a vertical hanging bag with plants of lettuce put on the side of the bag in holes, a system defined by DeKorne (1992–93). Another example is strawberry plants placed in perlite holes on the side of the vertical polyethylene bag. At the top of the bag, the nutrient solution is applied, usually via a dripper, and the solution goes down through the bag and out the bottom. The same issues with the NFT method apply to this device, as the nutrient solution composition is modified as it moves through the container.

A very recent unique system consists of a column of interlocking styrofoam pots in which plants are placed at the four corners of each pot; the system is designed primarily for the growth of strawberry, lettuce, and herbs. Nutrient solution positioning and flow are similar to the vertical sac system.

The use of vertical space is a benefit of these vertical systems, while maintaining lateral space if plants are grown in an enclosed shelter or greenhouse. The bag or column of pots can be slowly rotated to give the plants a more consistent light exposure.

Rockwool Slab Medium

Rockwool is possibly the most commonly used hydroponic growing medium for tomato, cucumber and pepper production in the world today, while attempts are being made to find an appropriate replacement because the disposal of the used slabs is becoming a major problem (Spillane, 2002a, b). Rockwool has excellent ability to retain water, is fairly inert, and has proven to be an excellent substratum for plant growth (Sonneveld, 1989).

Rockwool is an inert fibrous substance formed from a mixture of volcanic rock, calcareous and coke; melted between 1500 and 2000 C; extruded as fine fibers; pressed into loosely woven sheets. The sheets are made of slabs of varying widths [16 to 18 inches (15 to 46 cm)], usually 36 inches (91 cm) in length, and between 3 and 4 inches

(5 to 10 cm) in diameter. The slabs are usually covered with sheets of white polyethylene.

Usually, the slabs are laid flat on a prepared floor surface, which is then first covered with white polyethylene ground sheets. The spacing between the slabs will depend on the growth area configuration and the crop to be cultivated. After the slabs have been placed in place, cuts are made along the lower edge of each slab on the bottom of the polyethylene slab to allow excess nutrient solution to flow out of the slab. On top of the slab sheet, an access hole is then cut to accommodate a rockwool block which contains a growing plant. Using a drip irrigation system, the nutrient solution is then supplied to each rockwool block.

Since this is a "open" system, the nutrient solution is not recovered and the delivered solution is sufficient for an excess flow from the cut openings at the bottom of the slab. A solution sample is regularly drawn from the slab, its EC calculated, and if it is found to reach a certain amount, the slab is leached with water. A pH measurement may also be performed, and the composition of the nutrient solution may change if necessary. The elemental content of the slab-retained nutrient solution is not usually determined, although Ingratta et al. (1985) provided optimal and appropriate ranges for two crops, tomato and cucumber. Many inert substrates such as perlite will also be subject to these same values.

CHAPTER THREE

Hydroponic Pest Control: How to Protect Your Plants

If you're using hydroponics to do your planting, you're not at the same risk of plague infestation you're doing outdoors. You will do have other worries about protecting your plants from pests, though. Being cautious is a good thing, but avoidance of a pest problem before it occurs is much better. And here's what you need to know about regulation of hydroponic plague: the most every hydroponic plague problems. If you want to avoid pests, you need to learn what you may be dealing with first. Here are some of the most likely plagues you will find if you have pests in your system:

Aphids

Most people are familiar with aphids from classroom classes, so you thought you were done with them here. But they do infest hydroponic systems, especially when their food source contains too much nitrogen in your plants. They are usually found around the stems of the plant and these little guys can be black, green or grayish / tan.

Whitefly

Whiteflies can be tricky but you can easily spot them. They look like tiny white moths (approximately 1 mm long), and fly away as soon as you catch one.

Cat halibut

Spider mites are much smaller than whiteflies, with lengths below 1 mm. And they are certainly one of the hydroponic system's most feared infestations. They look like tiny spiders but they can easily avoid detection because they are so small before an infestation gets out of hand.

Gnats Fungus

The tricky pest is fungus gnats, because the produced gnat is not dangerous but the larvae are. You can find the insect larvae feeding at the roots which can easily cause bacterial infections.

Thrips

Thrips, like aphids, can turn yellow or brown leaves, since they suck out nutrients. At 5 mm they are a little bigger but still difficult to find. On the upper sides of the leaves they will look like tiny, black dots.

Avoid things that 'invite' pests to flourish in your area

There are some 'good practices' in your hydroponic system which can help reduce the chances of a pest making its home. Luckily, many of these activities require a little know-how, and a greater dose of evasion. That means one of the best things you can do is stop adding pest-appealing opportunities.

Don't go in dirty

You should wear sterile (or at least clean) clothes before you walk into your growing field. All kinds of bacteria, pests and other pollutants will cling totally unnoticed to our clothing. And if there's nothing in there you don't know, just don't gamble it. A pest problem is a high price to pay for skipping to get ready to reach your growing area for 2 minutes. Nonetheless, you have not yet done so, your equipment and all that you add to your through region require the same treatment.

Basically: Do not bring something that is not safe and contaminant-free into your expanding field.

Provide a sterile start to your system

When you set up your program, or you do some research on it, see the tip above. Even lights, pipes, tanks, and all other appliances need to be cleaned before they reach your through field. Time.

Also it is important to test the quality of the seals around your that field. While you want a well ventilated field, you don't want a pest free for all. Be sure that seals on windows and doors to outdoor areas are not an issue (especially when your growing area is close to outside vegetation).

Materials outside

Pests can grow from some sneaky places and the materials you put into your hydroponic garden are an unassuming place to hide. The plague home we mistakenly put into our hydroponic systems?

Cultivation Medium

Look, this is not to build a scare campaign because the reality is that the mediums that grow are perfectly sterile and healthy. But there are things to look for. Pay particular attention if you are having an organic growing medium, like coconut or rice husk. Those mediums can harbor pests, so special care is required. Make sure your rising medium has been sterilized, placed through pest elimination treatments, and have some reliable support behind those statements.

Fresh transplants

You need to be vigilant if you intend on adding transplants into your body. Plants outside can bear bacteria , fungi, disease and pests. You need to get some transplants from a safe, well-maintained place you can trust in to counter these risks. And only because it came from a 'reputable' factory, take the time to test the plants for any health problems, before you go transplanting it.

First steps in managing hydroponic pest

Pest control with your hydroponic system can be something you start experimenting with at the very beginning. In essence, putting steps to deter pests would be your first line of defense. Here are the best ways to avoid a plague problem:

Keeping the moisture

Many pests in other areas of your body, such as spider mites and fungus gnats, are especially attracted to low humidity and excess moisture. Holding the moisture from going too low (50 per cent is a reasonable amount for holding plants safe and keeping the mites away) will avoid infestation. But this isn't all about your surroundings. Keeping too much moisture from your growing medium will deter pests from taking up residence, such as fungus gnats (especially if you use rockwool they love).

How to spot a plague problem

You can still have a pest find its way into your system, even with vigilant prevention. As with any hydroponic set-up, you can periodically check your plants for issues. That said, you don't want to confuse pest symptoms with symptoms of other problems, such as nutrient deficiency or illness. Here's how to say whether your plants have rodents, or another ailment:

Discoloration:

When pests extract the nutrients from the leaves (as do aphids), you will find that the leaves are discolored and sometimes turn a yellow colour. This discoloration is focused around tiny holes from which the pests feed, and not just distributed over leaves in general.

Pitches and Spots

Some pests can leave spots with a signature pattern, be it white, yellow, brown or black. When you notice spots, check to see if they are leaf deposits (from eggs, feces, etc.), or actual leaf damage. If the spots scratch off you can guarantee you have a pest problem pretty well.

Test the leaves and stems of other plants to assess the plague and the degree of infestation when you find this on any plant.

Pest holes vs burns and lesions:

It can be quick to make conclusions when you see a hole or rip first. That's why closer look and check the edges of any holes is necessary. Burns will be relatively clear, because they should occur when light and heat sources are near to plants, and show discolouration around any holes or burns.

The pests most likely to infest hydroponic gardens are more 'suckers' than 'munchers.' That means the holes they leave from feeding on plants are small, mostly elevated and surrounded by a yellow, or whitish layer.

What to do when you have a pest?

If you've experienced any of the above pest-related symptoms, you need to get it fixed and quick. Unfortunately it can be difficult to minimize the problem when a pest has already found its way in. Pests can run at a startling pace through a hydroponic system, and if one plant is infected, the others appear to follow in a short time.

Don't wait to deal with a bug.

If you act right after spotting pests, you may be able to spare the rest of your plants (or remain unaffected). Unless you hesitate, you would definitely come home to a garden that has been infested almost, if not completely.

Determining the required level of intervention:

Some pests can be provided for through environmental improvements, manual removal or other approaches, and other pests can only be removed with chemicals. Evite the introduction of hazardous chemicals into your hydroponic system where appropriate.

More friendly pest control methods:

Sticky traps

One of the first things you can do is use sticky traps according to the pest you 're dealing with. These function like the other sticky bug traps you 're familiar with, and particularly pests that have short life cycles can be very helpful. Another advantage to using sticky traps is that they can help you to recognise the pests that infest your system. If you can locate the pests you can take a more suitable route to get rid of them (even if they are not removed by sticky traps).

Hint: Leaving traps sticky can also be a preventive measure. If you see pests trapped on a trap you can prevent a bigger problem.

Natural Solutions

A lot of strategies are being advertised to destroy pests, but you don't want to destroy your plants just by chance. When in doubt, make sure your solution is backed with plant safe guarantees. Pyrethrin is, without a doubt, a solution you can count on. It sounds very chemically intense, but don't worry. Even certified organic farmers have been given the green light to use so you know it's free. Pyrethrin is derived from chrysanthemums, so pests can be prevented.

Nice sprinkle down

You can often give a good hosting to your plants to start getting pests under control. True, it isn't going to kill all your pests, but it can disrupt another reproductive cycle and it's going to get the bulk of them off your plants.

Cheat sheet Hydroponic Pest Control:

If you encountered a pest problem that quickly becomes an emergency, here is the cheat sheet you need.

Symptoms:

- Black spots on leaves
- Deformed stems or leaves
- Deposits on leaves – for silvery streaks, small black, sticky residue, white masses and clumps
- Webbing around plants
- White or yellow spots

Pest information and treatment

Aphids

Aphids secrete honeydew, a sticky residue that stimulates sooty mold growth (honeydew can attract other pests, such as bees, too). Such creatures come out of leaves with these nutrients and can leave them looking yellow and crinkled.

Signs of Tell-tale:

Aphids leave behind a good honeydew deposit when they feed so these deposits are unlikely to miss you. Typically you can see the aphids flying along stems, but they can be a mix of colours.

Treatments:

To control their infestation, you can use predator bugs which feed on aphids; ladybugs and lacewings are the most common choices. Safe soap pesticides are formulated differently, but most are safe for plants and deadly for pests. Leaves, stems, or even whole, severely infested plants may need to be removed. Next, try not to overfeed your plants, because this will increase problems with the aphid.

Gnats Fungus

Adult fungus gnats are irritating (apart from the fact that they reproduce) but not a big concern. The larvae will be your main problem, as they gather nearby and feed on the roots.

Signs of Tell-tale:

The first sign that you may notice is the adult fungus gnats flying up in masses whenever you disturb a nearby area. You can find the larvae by looking at the growing medium, and turning it over a little. The plants they feed on in the beginning look 'bad,' meaning they get yellow leaves, look wilted and look fragile.

Treatments:

Second, stop these guys by trying not to overwater your plants; but if you have already reached that level, try to let the growing medium dry out as soon as possible, a few inches from the surface before adding any more humidity.

You can capture eggs near the medium with sticky traps, and add nematodes for the larvae to take care of. Even Neem oil can be sprayed for serious infestations.

Wheat Bugs

Mealybugs enjoy fruiting plants and you are more likely to see them if you grow the way you are. These are another form of 'sucker' insect, so if an infestation gets bigger you'll find thin, yellow leaves.

Signs of Tell-tale:

Mealybugs leave eggs in thin, cotton-looking masses on the undersides of leaves and stems (although on the plants they make themselves located anywhere). They leave behind a residue of honeydew, much like aphids, and tend to have a waxy coating.

Treatments:

Solutions: A gentle, natural pesticide or insecticide will address Mealybug problems. Additionally, you can use 1 oz Neem oil solution with 1 gallon of water and spray every 1 or 2 weeks until the infestation is over. It is possible to use certain helpful insects such as ladybugs too.

Tip: You can manually dissolve egg sacks with a swab soaked in alcohol when you spot an infestation early, and then kill them.

Cat halibut

Spider mites leave fine webs around plants, and can be a tough pest. They prefer to infest areas with a low humidity and high temperatures.

Signs of Tell-tale:

Firstly, websites. Spider mites, much like normal spiders, leave behind sticky webs but smaller and finer. You can note yellow and whitish spots on leaves, since they often suck nutrients from leaves. Once you find webs, they will develop in number quickly so check the undersides of the leaves where they are collecting.

Treatments:

Firstly, by pruning and cutting highly infested leaves and stems, manually avoid areas of high infestation. A healthy, organic insecticide or biological insecticide can then be used to get it under control. You may also spray a mixture of Neem oil and a wetting agent (for better spread) every few days to destroy the mites and eggs.

Tricks

Thrips can grow large populations in a short span of time, and if left untreated, a heavy infestation will cripple a plant. These hyperactive pests are particularly attracted to plants and flowers of light colour.

Signs of Tell-tale:

One of the main signs that you have a problem with thrip is the black spots on the leaves. The black spots are in fact feces that are dropped onto leaves. You'll also notice that they get discolored spots on the plants they feed on and may seem dry.

Treatments:

To get rid of thrips, the first thing you can do is release some insects that feed on them. Lacewings and ladybugs are typical beneficial bugs but when it comes to thrips, minute pirate bugs are most successful. If the issue is too severe, pyrethrin can be used and followed when appropriate with an insecticide soap.

Whitefly

Whiteflies hide on the leaves' undersides, and look like miniature moths. Like fungus gnats, when disturbed, they fly up into large crowds.

Signs of Tell-tale:

Unlike aphids, whiteflies leave a sticky trace of honeydew which you can spot on the leaves (as well as any sooty mold which has formed as a result). You can also see small, discolored spots fed on leaves by whiteflies. When an adult population is created, you should be able to say easily if they are within your system.

Treatments:

To start raising the infestation, spray plants at moderate pressure with water, and start introducing beneficial insects. Like other pests, they can be minimized by using ladybugs and lacewings, as well as the whitefly parasite.

Natural soap insecticides will easily get rid of them, just as Neem oil spray would.

How To Build A Deep Water Culture System

Deep water culture systems are among the most cost-effective and open hydroponic systems any gardener can operate. The required materials are straightforward yet there are numerous ways to build these DWC systems.

These systems can be bought, but it is worth any growers time to create one and use it as a learning resource for future projects, since they are so easy to install. There we'll go through what exactly is DWC, the advantages and drawbacks of this type of system, and what this type of hydroponic system takes to construct.

DWC System Types

There's the usual DWC program, and the one we 're going to concentrate on here. There are also a few other styles worth noting. In architecture they are very similar but with a few slight variations.

Method Kratky

It can be almost the same in design as a standard DWC system except not using an air pump. The entire system is passive and does not have any extra features or facilities.

The way this system works is to leave a gap between the surface and the roots of your nutrient mix. It will be half a condition in which half of the roots will be exposed, and the other half will be inundated. The roots will grow longer as the water levels drop, and follow it down.

RDWC (The Deep Water Culture Recirculating System)

Such DWC recirculating systems are used when the scaling problems occur. It is impossible to efficiently scale down regular DWC systems. These operate as a cross between DWC and Drain and Flood systems, but with one distinction. The nutrients never drip out of the growing area.

This works by making several containers or seals all attached to a central reservoir. It helps you to scale, as it only includes adding additional buckets. In practice, the oxygenated water in turn transits from the reservoir to each plant before returning to the reservoir.

Depending on the variety there should be enough growing space in each bucket for either 2 or 3 plants. Also, if you have more than that, there may be competition between your plants for the nutrients and the oxygen.

Bubbleponics

This system is almost the same as a standard DWC system and the only difference is to have a water pump attached. That sits inside the reservoir and pumps the oxygenated water to the top of the net cups where your plants rest. It then flows back into the reservoir through the rising medium, and cascades.

This type of system of bubbleponics is optimal when the plants are small, and their roots do not touch the reservoir water. If they are long enough and can get to the solution on their own, this form of system has no advantages over a standard DWC system.

Items Needed to Build a DWC System

- A source of water and nutrients
- Net DWC jars to carry your plants
- Nutrient hydroponics and pH-adjusters
- Air pump and air stones for tank aeration

Here is a little more detail on each of the components:

DWC Reservoir

In a DWC device the roots of the plant would be suspended in the net pots from above. Their rooting systems will reach down to immersing themselves in the solution. This type of system may have reservoirs for each plant, or you have multiple plants that share the same reservoir.

If plants share the same reservoir, growing different plants together could be challenging. Reservoirs for single plants offer more flexibility and control.

The reservoir may be any obscure container that has a lid. You'll cut through big enough holes in this to accommodate your net tanks. Then, these pots are filled with rising medium.

It should be noted that no light should be permitted to get inside because this can lead to algae growth and as the roots would be exposed, if the light is there for long periods, they may fall foul of air pruning.

The tubes should be modified to black instead of clear plastic when you mount your air pump, because this will support algae growth which will spread deeper into the tank. You should also check where the lid sits on top of the tank and can seal it with plumbers tape if needed.

One helpful tip that some growers do to cover a reflective material at the top of the tank. This not only stops the tank from being heated by ambient light but also helps to reflect light back on the underside of your plants.

Net Pots for DWC

The difference between net pots and standard pots is that they have no solid component, instead they are a mesh where the roots can move easily to enter the solution below them. You can make your own net pots, but since these are so cheap, it's easier to stick to the net pots you can purchase.

In addition, your pots will be the placeholder for your inert growing medium with low water retention properties. Clay pebbles (Hydroton) are ideal for this, as they allow the roots to reach maximum airflow. You will need to germinate your seeds before planting into these. These are more likely to be in cubes of Rockwool which you can move once they are large enough.

Note: There's no way the roots will be long enough to reach the solution within the reservoir when you first transplant your seedlings. You'll need to top-water your plants for the first few days.

You can also ensure your Rockwool cubes reach the nutrient solution surface. This way they can wick up the water until they can take the roots directly from the surface.

Hydroponic Nutrients

You'll need to keep an eye on your pH levels using a DWC system. The range will be between 5.5 and 6.5 with 5.8 being the optimal reading. One benefit of a DWC system is that you can potentially use less nutrients than in other system forms, but you need to control the pH levels carefully all the time.

It is here that the pH UP and pH Down come into play.

Another thing to remember is your EC / pppm ratios, as this will let you know your nutrient concentrations. When you learn to flush the machine this will be important. Once you understand the needs of your plant, you can find that you can expand through a whole without altering the solution, and topping off the reservoir depends only on the amount of nutrients they use.

DWC Aeration

Plants need oxygen to grow, and although receiving some through the clay pebbles, it's not going to be enough to support them. Any DWC system can have air pumps as one of the most important components. Choosing an air pump which has no less than 2 outlets is recommended. It will allow you to place air stones in separate sections of your tank to provide plenty of oxygen.

The air pump model you select will provide enough oxygen to the water. A strong guide is one which can produce the volume of your reservoir twice the liters per hour. That means if you have a 100 liter tank, then you need an air pump that can supply 200 liters of air per hour.

It's worth remembering that this air pump works around the clock to keep the solution well-aerated. When this fails, then you will see your plants quickly die.

You can buy a dissolved oxygen meter if you want to calculate the concentrations of oxygen in your water. The better and more accurate ones are not inexpensive, so it should be sufficient to generate as much oxygen as you can, instead of calculating the amounts you think you have. Such systems are ideally suited for industrial growers.

How Does DWC Work?

Plants don't take too kindly to have their roots plunged into water, and they can get suffocated. This will in many cases lead to death. But why is it different in a DWC method, because the plants submerge their roots in water 24/7?

The Oxygen is the secret to their survival. That is where the air pump comes into play as it gives the water sufficient quantities of oxygen. You may also use air pumps in other hydroponic systems, or falling water in a circulation system may add oxygen to the water.

In DWC systems, while soaking up the nutrients, plants will take the dissolved oxygen from the water at the same time. In fact this makes them grow much faster than if they were in the soil.

You'll add your water and nutrient mix to your tank, this will be balanced to the optimal range by pH. If you have this, you'll then suspend your plants in the net pots that protruding through the reservoir cover.

You will be using the air pump at this point, and when selecting the right air pump for your system , make sure that you have one with several nozzles. It will allow you to position more air stones, or you can use multiple reservoirs with one pump.

If the roots are sufficiently long to enter the nutrient solution, then their growth can burst.

This works because plants need to look for tiny pockets of water in the soil, and all they need in a DWC system is right underneath them. You may think you've got so many air bubbles when in fact, the better it's for your plants the more you can have.

DWC Pros and Cons

It's important to see the pros and cons that come with them in order to better grasp how these DWC systems are operating.

Pros

- Speedier plant growth due to increased nutrient uptake and water oxygen. A perfect example of this is lettuce. This can be grown in around 30 days when grown in soil, compared with 60 days.

- There are very few moving components – in many cases only the air pump exists

- There are not as many nutrients or fertilizers needed because the roots are submerged in the nutrient mix.

- Once a DWC system is up and running, very little maintenance is necessary. As there are few moving parts or water in circulation, nothing can become obstructed or blocked

With DWC systems, all isn't rosy and they do have some downsides. Fortunately though, the upsides outweigh the bad points by quite a sizeable amount.

Cons

- In smaller DWC systems, it can be possible to wrongly calibrate the nutrients, this can be either way.

- When a power outage or pump failure happens, it will be a matter of hours before the plants drown to low oxygen levels.

- Large variations can be seen in your nutrient mixes. That can include levels of water and pH.

- If you are using a non-circulating DWC system, it can be difficult to maintain an optimal temperature.

As you can see, most of the trouble areas stem from the lack of air to the solution. If you can prepare for this then the chance of plants dying will be reduced. Which is why some farmers have backup air pumps in case this happens.

Lighting for DWC Systems

This will focus on where your DWC machine is working. If you have access to sunlight then there are more than enough natural periods. However, if you are developing indoors, this is very different because you need to take into account the heat that will produce your lighting.

Additional lighting can only operate for a maximum of 16 hours a day, as plants need time to rest, and 8 hours of darkness is more than adequate.

The combined heat of any pumps and lighting must be considered, and the effect it has on your water temperature. If you are using HID lights, this may be the case you need a small chiller unit. You may be able to get away with T5 fluorescents depending on your plant form, because these run much hotter, and your water temperature may not be too much affected.

Common Questions Asked About DWC Systems

Which DWC Form Will I Try First?

If you're an absolute novice then it's probably best to start with either a traditional DWC system or you can try a Kratky system if you don't want to commit right away. These types are both plain and inexpensive to set up. Even though they may seem the simplest in nature, they still can produce excellent yields.

What nutrients do I need to use in My DWC?

Many farmers prefer to use organic types of nutrients, and although these yield excellent results, it is advisable to stick to nutrients that are known to function and can be modified easily.

General Hydroponics 3-part system is more than suitable and can be easily modified to match a wide variety of plants to various ratios. These are also fairly cheap and have proven to work well.

How deep will the roots be going into the water?

When transplanting your seedlings or topping off your reservoir, you can make sure that only the bare root is immersed in the mud. Your plants stem should be kept exposed. Around 1.5 inches of roots will be outside of the water level.

These exposed sections of the root system allow your plates to absorb even more oxygen from surrounding plants.

What Is My Reservoir Temperature To Be?

Temperature can be one of the drawbacks of DWC systems as we have seen. If you grow indoors and have a circulation system, the heat and heat from your growing lights will be produced by the pump. If the mixture of nutrients is too warm it will reduce the amount of oxygen in the water. On the other side, if you cool your mixture, and it gets too cold, it can cause stunted growth of plants.

The ambient air temperatures should be around 75 – 80F, and for optimum development, the temperatures around the root zone must be between 60 – 68F.

What the Ideal pH and EC / PPM would be for DWC?

The suggested pH level range is from 5.5 to 6.5. This will depend on the type of plant and the stage of growth of your plants though.

It is normal for vegetative crops to have higher-end pH levels, while fruit or flowering plants may need a lower-end pH level.

It is recommended that you combine lower nutrient levels in DWC systems when you start looking at the EC levels. There are only a few explanations for this. First, if your water doesn't move, the concentration is all in one location and that's directly exposed to the roots of your plant.

Furthermore, plants suck up more water than nutrients so that the nutrient content in your solution can be increased as the levels decrease, thereby providing a higher EC. This can be more damaging to your plants if you apply maximum pressure. Adding lower rates does not automatically harm them, it just means they'll work a little harder to learn what they need.

It is really easy to set up a DWC program, whether it's one that's bought or one that's installed by yourself. The results would be the same and with minimum effort, these are high yields from your plants. Another advantage of a DWC system is that if you have spare space, it can be used as a supplementary device, they require so little effort to operate that even the smallest spaces can be used.

Anyone wanting to try hydroponics should first try one of those systems. There's nothing to lose but there's plenty to win as a grower.

CHAPTER FIVE

How to Germinate Seeds for Hydroponics: Step-By-Step

One of the most important steps in an often neglected hydroponic garden is getting the plants first. There's plenty of discussion on pH and nutrient levels, but these are only appropriate for established gardens.

An up and running system is very different from a germination field, and with the pace at which some plants can grow, you can need to constantly germinate your seeds to keep your garden filled with new plants for growth.

Many people skip this step and buy seedlings which they can drop right into their system. Although this is more convenient, it does mean that you might be limited to what you can expand.

Your plants should avoid any trauma, injury or disease transmission when developing from seeds as if they were grown in soil or other media and then transplanted into your system from an outside environment.

The thing that many growers forget is that they can get a lot more seed for the seedlings price it costs.

While germination of seeds and seedlings can be relatively easy, and nature will do some of the hard work for you, there are a few bits of equipment you need to learn, words you need to learn, and some practical steps you need to take to get the best germination rate.

If you start germinating from your own seeds first, it will be a little more costly due to the equipment you need to buy, but once you're on your way, this expense can be easily offset by the amount of plants you will grow from seeds.

Hydroponic Germination Basics

One thing to remember right at the outset is that seeds will germinate in soil, but they are advised not to do so. This is only for a few reasons. Bacteria can be moved from the soil to your hydroponic system and, second, it will affect the roots of your seedlings because they will need to wash before they are transplanted. Use a dedicated growing medium such as Rockwool or Coco coir / Coco peat is much safer for this.

Another thing worth noting is that there are many sites where seeds are labeled as Hydroponic Seeds, there is no need to look for that as every seed is appropriate for use in a hydroponic system.

Steps of Seed Germination

They start in a dormant state when seeds begin to germinate, and then, as they develop, they enter an active growing stage.

This process contains 5 pieces, which can be seen here:

- Seed coat-this is the seed's rough outer shell
- Plumule-these are the embryo plant's first shoots or stems
- Hypocotyl – this is the portion below the seed leaf stalks that sits directly above the root system

- Radicle-this is the first root

- Cotyledon – these are the embryonic leaves that grow in plants which produce seeds. There will be one or more of the first leaves from germinating seeds that you can see. This help in retaining nutrients before more dominant leaves begin to develop.

The Radicle will crack as the dormant state comes to an end, and from this, there will be an early shot. The seeds need to be in dry moist conditions for this to happen. The Cotyledons job is to provide the seeds with their first nutrients, which they will usually get from the soil, but there is no chance for them to do so in hydroponic systems.

Propagation is the name given to the process in which seedlings begin to gain energy, and when they grow stronger roots and their first real leaves. This growth process starts as plants emerge from the seed, and ends as they produce roots that have grasped the germination plug within.

If two or three sets of real leaves have been formed by plants this is the stage where they can be transplanted into the system.

Equipment Needed for Hydroponic Seed Germination

Although you can use a few types of growing medium to germinate seeds, it's worth running through them to see how they work in your hydroponic garden.

Coco Peat

This that medium is a by-product of the cocoa cultivation industry. It comes from the coir fibers and is washed and heat processed before being converted into peat coconut products. You'll see that most often in the form of big bricks.

The special properties of this medium are, it is sterile, and it has normal rooting hormones. This also has antimicrobial properties despite being 100 percent organic. Coco peat can be used anywhere you'd used peat moss before. Other properties include that it can keep its own weight in water 8-9 times.

Coco peat can store and release nutrients to plants for extended periods, and it provides fantastic properties for oxygenation. Normal coconut peat pH levels are 5.0-6.8, so it is neutral and slightly acidic bordering. The one downside to using Coco Peat is that you will wash some of the loose particles inside your body. It can lead to blockages in pumps and sludge in reservoirs.

Coco Coir

This rising medium derives from the same processes as coconut peat but it is not ground into fine powder. It differs because the hairs found on the husks of coconut are the ones. This is most widely used in passive hydroponic systems, but it can also be used for later use in your system in the form of starter cubes or larger cubes.

Coco coir comes with all the same characteristics as coco peat and is an outstanding growing medium all over but can suffer from the same downside. Coco coir is not waterproof, and mud can be washed off leading to the same pump clogs and buildup of reservoir sludge. Before use, it can be rinsed to remove any of those loose particles.

Rockwool

This rising medium is not normal, and is rendered into thin threads by heating and spinning different silica-based materials. This is the same method that is used to create roof insulation, and should be handled with the same care during use.

Rockwool provides an ideal material which, although being pH neutral, has an almost perfect oxygen to water ratio when used. Most often it comes in the form of 1-inch square cubes or plugs which are ideal for starting your seeds.

If these are germinating on their way, they are quickly transplanted into larger cubes that have a pre cut hole to accommodate the plug. Also perfect for transplantation into other the media, the smaller plugs are suitable for NFT, drip, and deep water culture systems.

Rockwool growth cubes possess a pH of about 7.8 which is a little alkaline.

These three media can be interchangeable but we will use Rockwool as the point of reference for the remainder of this article.

It needs to be noted, because Rockwool is like insulating materials, it can make you itch, or it can be harmful to breathe the fibers. You just have to handle this material as much as necessary without any unnecessary touching.

Other required items

- Containers which can hold water, Germination tray with dome
- Chemicals used to increase or lower pH
- Seeds to choose from
- Lights expand if they germinate indoors
- Heating pad in case of lower temperatures than needed

Germinating Seeds Using Rockwool

Step 1: Hydrating and Stabilizing

You may need one or more containers, depending on the number of seeds you are looking for to germinate. These must be big enough to carry your Rockwool cubes after they've been soaked in water.

If the water level is too high, the seeds can drown due to the excess water. The seed must be at a height where the water canwick the cube up to the seed, but from above, there is also air available for the seed.

You may use distilled water at this early stage, or standard faucet water. Everyone must work on an equal basis with each other. Once the water is in your bottle, you may need to check the pH levels. There are a few growers who suggest adding half strength or lower nutrient solution, but it's not appropriate at this point, and the seeds won't gain that much, and in some cases they died once nutrients are applied to the sprouting seeds.

Take a read using either a pH test kit or a pH test meter. It that read up or down depending on the type of water you use, but you may notice that the water gives a 7.4 reading. This means you'll need to use your pH down solution to lower the pH.

The pH that you need to strive for is as close as you can to 5.5-6. You should not let the pH drop to below 5.5 at any point. When this happens, the Rockwool fibers may get harmed.

Insert the starter cubes and allow them to soak for about an hour. At this time they'll swell at soaking up the bottle water.

Rockwool cubes are capable of keeping the optimal air to water balance ratio. When unwanted squeezing happens, this will change the ratio and can cause cube deformation. The cubes will stay wet for several days without any further watering.

When you pre soak the cubes in pH equilibrated water before moving them to another tray. Do not waste the water, just hold it for later in a sealed container.

Step 2: Planting Seeds into the Cubes

Depending on your Rockwool cube manufacturer, you may have the ones that already come in the cubes without holes. If this is the case, what you need to do is make a hole in the top that is no more than a quarter of an inch deep down to a depth.

Now, all you need to do is take a few seeds and put them carefully into the opening. They do not fall to the bottom so you'll need a small tool to move them gently to the bottom of the hole. Once completed, you can move another small piece of Rockwool gently into the hole to cover the seeds. Be sure that this is only close enough to prevent light from entering.

It may seem backward but what you are doing now is covering the jar. It will leave the seeds in darkness, which will maintain moisture and avoid evaporation as well. It is this climate that is essential to proper germination of seeds.

You can buy dedicated germination trays that come with plastic domes, that's not necessary. Many growers often slip their trays inside a Ziploc bag to hold moisture, but this means your trays are going to be much smaller. All you need is an upgraded tray of the same size or something you can sit across the tray without pushing on the cubes of Rockwool.

No matter what you use to cover your tray, whether it's a Ziploc or a plastic sheet, your trays need to stay in the dark during the time of germination. The area where your seed trays are laid will be about 68F, if your growing / nursery area is less than this, this is where the heating pad is used. It's going to be perfect a few degrees above but it's below that really causes the problems.

Step 3: Let Nature Take its Course

While in this process the seeds germinate, you need to test the water levels daily depending on how warm your climate is. That is one of the benefits of using Rockwool as during that time you might find that they don't need any, or limited watering.

From the first step, this is where you will use the reserved water, simply add enough to keep the blocks moist as water levels drop.

This is also why at this point, it is advisable not to add any nutrients. Sprouts are getting stronger, and require nutrients only when they're in your system.

You may find that both have sprouted when you added more than one seed to each hole (there would be mortality rates or slow growers). Trying to delete the one and replant it will be tempting but you should stop doing this. It may cause damage to the rooting system of other sprouts.

Depending on the rising conditions, this stage is usually reached in about 3-4 days. Once you see the first true leaves appearing, it's time to pick the bigger of the two shoots and cut off the bigger one with the cube's top edge. Unfortunately, it is a choice you need to make.

It is time for plants to start receiving light once they have reached this stage to help them grow. Most people use sun-facing windows to provide this light, and while it is perfect for initial illumination, it can cause issues later.

Whether using the sun or rising lights, it is the red-light level that will promote the development of seedlings. Three hours a day is enough when using the sun, and the periods that include most of the red light are between 6am and 9am or later in the early evening from about 4 p.m. to 6 p.m.

Using the window method would involve turning of the trays so that the seedlings won't lean towards the sun. Moreover, as your seedlings get bigger they will need up to 15 hours of light a day.

That is where a sun-facing window leads to difficulties, maybe there isn't enough light. If this occurs, and seedlings obtain inadequate light, they develop weakly and leggily. When this happens, they start falling over, and in certain situations, it's something from which they can not recover.

Overhead grow lights solve this issue because you can set the timer for 15 hours a day, and the seedlings won't lean to the side because the lights are overhead. Additionally they can grow much stronger and safer as they obtain a complete quota of light.

Another thing to remember is that seedlings need time to recover from light so the nursery area will have enough darkness when they have their quota.

One more warning is to ensure that any growing lights are placed far enough from the top of the seedlings, so that they are not scorched (depending on the type of light). As they expand, they'll need to raise the lights. Watering may become more regular as the seedlings begin to take in more fluids, especially if your lighting fixtures have heat.

Step 4: Transplanting

The first steps of germination can take about 2-3 weeks to when you can transplant into your system.

You should test the bottoms of your Rockwool cubes instead of waiting for this time limit, and when you see the roots start protruding from the bottom, then you can transplant. This can be a positive sign because they will start to get root bound in the cube if you leave them too long, because that would be their only source of moisture.

Upon reaching this point, you can clear up room for your new young plants in your system. Along with the Rockwool cube, you can move the entire plant into your rising media where you can lightly cover the surface.

Since the plant rooting mechanism has been centered on the cube for moisture, it needs a chance to look for another water source naturally, so you can overwater them for the first few days to allow them to do that.

Why Haven't all My Seedlings Survived?

There are several explanations why not all seedlings can survive that can't be explained to all. But there are temperature variations which must be accounted for depending on the plants being grown. If you have cold weather plants and warm weather plants in the same climate as seedlings, then it may be too much temperature change for either plant form.

Other things you need to be cautious about are:

- Media drying out-seeds need to germinate in a wet, humid climate. This can kill them if they dry in between watering, or prevent them from sprouting.

- Keep high humidity – this is necessary if moisture is to stay. Humidity domes or an upturned tray will help retain moisture and humidity on top of your grow tray. It will also be beneficial to have a transparent dome while under lights.

- Too damp – if you get too damp over water or your Rockwool cubes, the seeds can rot before they germinate properly. You can spray inside your rising tray, rather than pouring water, to ensure you don't overwater. Many growing trays have ridged the bottoms, so that the rising cubes do not stand in stagnant water. If a situation happens too wet, you can get what's called damping off. Here, during the propagation process, a few molds and fungi develop and cause the seedlings to lose their stem structure and lay flat.

• Do not overfeed – this will only be when you start feeding on nutrients when you see the first sets of true leaves. Your water's EC will be max. 0.8 – 1.2. Plants can get all their nutrients from the cotyledons during the early stages of life, and it is only when these first true leaves show they are dependent on external nutrient or fertilizer sources.

Transplanting Tips

It can seem like a simple exercise but plants will be susceptible to transplant shock at this point. It is not only because of the stresses of being separated from the through tray but also because it is put in a new setting. This initial shock can take several hours for them to recover from.

The seedlings are responsive to heat, and even more so when transplanted. This will include their new life under stronger lighting but also your nutrient mix temperature.

The best time to transplant is when you're about to water your seedlings. The growing cubes will be slightly damp, and your growing tray will have shrunk down a bit. This will make it easier for them to remove and to position them in a facility that has running water when they do.

Seed Tips

Although there are lots of germination-friendly seeds, some more exotic plant seeds do have special requirements. Here's a quick overview of what you might find on seed quest.

Pre-soak seeds – some growers suggest that seeds should be pre soaked before germination. This will make it easier to saturate the seed coat, and split open. Though, as hydroponic germination methods relative to soil are in the mid 90 percent, this is not recommended unless the speeds explicitly require soaking.

Scarification – several fruit plant seeds can require a weakening of their exterior before germination. In nature, that's animal or bird feature. To mimic this in hydroponics, some form of scarification will be required of this type of seed. This may involve the seeds running over a metal disk, rubbed over sandpaper, smashed with a hammer gently or even sliced with a knife. If you have any seeds of this kind, be sure to conduct this process only on the seeds that you will use. When scarified they're not going to store very well.

Seed inhibitors – since some seeds are supposed to lay dormant during the winter period, they have built-in inhibitors which prevent them from germinating too early. Some of the inhibitors can be found in Abscisic acid pathway. When winter comes to an end, this will decrease in seeds, because the seeds are ready to sprout. To resolve this, this type of seed can be placed in a moist growing medium and put in a refrigerator for four weeks. This cycle is called stratification, and by doing so enzymes break down and mimic what is happening in the wild. This process will require temperate native plants which need this winter season. It may be rare but learning how you can work around it is useful.

Phenolic compounds are another toxin which can be found in desert plants. This prevents the seeds from germinating before ample moisture is available, this inhibitor is water-soluble, and once it has been broken down, the seed can then sprout. All it requires is enough moisture for these to sprout.

Temperature – We've talked about temperature, but the upper heat limits are worth mentioning because this can prevent seeds from germinating, or even killing them. When the rising media increases above 90F then it is unlikely you will see any action. You can test this very easily with a hydroponic thermometer. It occurs in many situations in greenhouses where growers germinate but it is important to have the optimal temperature.

CHAPTER SIX

Vegetables You Can Grow With Hydroponics

Hydroponics is a booming means of growing domestic produce. New gardeners who think of this also wonder what are the best crops to grow, which are easy to grow and will produce the best yields.

There are many reasons why people turn to this way of rising, and it doesn't matter if it's because they want to help save the world or cut their grocery bill down on it. Hydroponics is a smart way of doing this, and more.

While not all vegetables grow in a hydroponic climate, many do. So here's the end, nine new hydroponic cultivators will develop into their system. Others are quite simple, while others require a little more effort and space, but they are all worth adding to any hydroponic garden.

Here we will look at each of these top nine hydroponic vegetables, and which systems are ideally suited to growing them.

Best Vegetables for Hydroponics

Lettuce

The leaf lettuce makes hydroponic cultivation an excellent choice. In simplest systems it develops and needs minimal attention. You can harvest the outer leaves from your lettuce as you grow, meaning you'll end up with a prolonged crop of fresh, crunchy lettuce. As the leaves are cut, the leaves within will quickly grow to take their place.

Many varieties are available to choose from, and most of them are ideal for growing this way. The forms which are more popular are:

- Tom Thumb.
- At Boston
- Mary

- New York City

- Romana

- The Bibb Buttercrunch

- Simpson

- The Deep Green Waldman

Lettuce is ideal for rising in NFT, DWC and Ebb and Flow systems. If they get too hot on the temperature, lettuce will bolt and taste bitter. They are a vegetable from the cold weather and prefer temperatures between 50 and 70 degrees fahrenheit. Lettuce are also fond of high levels of nitrogen.

Kale

Kale is one of the top vegetables grown for its health benefits and is delicious in taste. This may germinate from seeds and can handle a wide range of temperatures from 45 to 85 degrees fahrenheit once it starts growing.

It takes about ten weeks from seed to harvest, but like lettuce, you can pluck up to 30 per cent of the leaves of the plant. Again, there will be new leaves growing back and you can extend the time your crops are in your system. You will cut down on harvesting time to around

6 weeks if you transplant. One good thing about kale when grown indoors is that it's not attacked by many pests. The primary culprit being the aphids, but they may suffer from powdery mildew.

Curly kale (a common type sold in grocery stores), Lacinato kale (sweeter and with longer leaves), and Red Russian Kale are the main varieties. This variety has a reddish appearance and is the sweetest you can grow.

Spinach

Being another cool weather crop, this is ideal for growing along with kale and lettuce. Any temperature above a fahrenheit of 75 degrees would see the plant suffer. This can be grown from seeds and for up to three weeks before planting, many hydroponic growers can put their seeds in the refrigerator. This makes a more stable plant and thus a better plant. However, since they are cool weather plants, they do like around 12 hours of light a day, T5 fluorescent lamps might be the best lighting choice.

You should lower the temperatures when it's almost time to harvest as that has the effect of making the crop sweater. Growth will slow though, because of this. In order to prevent a bitter tasting herb, it is advisable to go for quality over quantity.

Most systems are ideal for spinach, but just remember to plant them a couple of weeks apart so that you can harvest continuously. For these can be a raft system ideal because it can also be for lettuce and kale.

Cucumbers

Growing cucumber can be so satisfying in the hydroponics. These vegetables are fond of the conditions given to them. Warmth, good for nutrients and plenty of moisture. Growers are amazed at the yields as they quickly become one of the most productive vegetables you can grow.

The optimal temperatures for maximum growth are just beyond the ranges like the greens that are leafy above. They will expand within a range of 60 to 82 degrees fahrenheit, saying this. This makes them perfect to grow alongside the two next crops on the list.

Cucumber likes a pH of 5.8 with an EC of 1.8 to 2. Growers can consider seeds costly for a good hybrid variety, but this cost per seed is more than justified when you see what fruits one seed can carry once it's developing.

The hardest thing about cucumber growth is that they are plants for wine making and need trellises. This makes them more suitable for flooding and drainage or other bucket type structures, where there is plenty of increasing medium to assist with support. That being said, coconut coir is one of the best mediums to use so long as the plants are well protected.

Look out for such pests as mites, thrips, whiteflies, and aphids. Such insects love to manipulate the cucumber crops.

Grape tomatoes

This shows that as growers move on to tomatoes they appreciate their method and wish to go on to the next level. What hydroponics is all about is getting a continuous supply of new tomatoes.

They are a plant with warm weather, and prefer temperatures prefer cucumbers. However, they prefer an EC level that starts at 2 and goes up to 5, so they need to separate some method to allow tomatoes to grow on their own, or at least with other plants that like this level.

The optimal pH is between 5.5 and 6.5 and the fahrenheit is between 58 and 79 degrees. Most probably the upper end of the scale.

They can be planted from seeds, but cuttings or seedlings are preferred since growing fruiting plants from seeds takes too long. There are several different styles, but the vineyards are common as they are easier to manage and harvest from.

Tomatoes as if cucumbers need trellises so that they can grow upwards, and they will produce a steady stream of fresh fruits that you can part harvest from.

Tomatoes can be affected by various pests and diseases such as spider mites, aphids, mosaic virus, and more. Another thing that can happen depending on the variety of tomatoes is that they may be susceptible to splits. This is when the tomato 's interior is rising faster than the exterior. It also occurs in a short time, because they suck up too much space.

Rabbits

While most root vegetables aren't ideal for hydroponic growth, radish is different. These are a cool crop from the weather so they can complement the first few plants on the list. They also mature quickly, and it just happens that they are one of the easiest plants to grow.

The pH is bets about 6 to 7, with temperatures range from 50 to 65 degrees fahrenheit. When you grow a longer radish variety these can withstand a little more heat than the types of short bulbs. EC levels are expected to fall from 1.6 to 2.2.

The lighting requirements are limited and require at least 6 hours. Between 8 and 10 hours of light are optimal.

We do not suggest seedlings, because they are best grown from seeds. It can take as little as three or four weeks from germination to harvest. Add to that, you can reap all the way through the year if you stagger your planting. In hydroponic systems where the temperature hovers between 72-76 degrees Fahrenheit this cool-weather crop grows excellent.

The most common radish problem is that if they are not held mist they can easily bolt, and if they're too wet they can suffer from root rot.

Bovines

In a hydroponic garden almost any sort of bean can be grown. There are hundreds of runners, string, pole beans and bush beans to choose from and the most popular are. These are easy to sustain and highly competitive for the effort that goes into growing them. Other styles require more effort as they climb / wine plants and they will need trellises for help.

They are fast germinators when developing from seed, and can take less than two weeks. Some varieties can even start in as little as seven days.

When they grow and you can see that they have two true leaves, they are the right size for going into your garden. However, a drip system is also possible, depending on the device form, while ebb and flow is the better choice. When plants are the bush type, they should be planted about 4-inch apart. Pole beans can be lined up a little wider at about 6 inches apart.

One positive thing about beans is they pollinate themselves. Growing medium should be loose so hydroton pebbles, or a combination of perlite and vermiculite, are good options and have many benefits. Perlite does not impact the levels with a neutral pH and expanded clay pebbles does give the roots adequate moisture and oxygen.

It is enough for twelve or thirteen hours of light and the normal temperatures will be between 70 and 80 degrees fahrenheit. If a temperature drops below 60, or rises above 60, then the plants pod growth will have a knock-on effect.

Beans don't require many nutrients so you can have a continuous harvest by spreading them apart when planting. For growing plant this will arrive in as little as 50 days.

Peppers

Peppers are an excellent addition because they can be grown in any season. Not only this, but growers will experience yields that are far greater than if they are grown by traditional means. This means that fruits are bigger and better quality as the plants are delivered what they need to enable them to grow to their genetic potential.

Ebb and flow systems are ideally suited for this type of crop, although they can be grown comfortably in others that have a strong base of growing media for support. These plants can grow very large, so they need a further spacing between plants of between 7 and 9 inches. That can limit a pot to just two plants.

Light needs to be about six to eight inches above the plants and need to be changed when they ripen. It can cause scorching if the bulbs are closer than this, and if further away it can affect the yield or potential production.

Lighting will be up to 12 hours a day, and no less than 10 hours. In addition, they'll also need enough nighttime hours. Regular temperatures have to be between 73 and 80 degrees fahrenheit, so they are ideal companions to be with tomatoes and cucumbers.

During their development, extra attention is needed where stem buds need pruning, since the plants are about 8-inch long. It makes the plant devote its resources to growing fruits than other smaller ones.

The pH levels must be between 5.5 and 7, and the EC will be within the 3 to 3.5 range.

Celery

Celery may be one of the toughest vegetables to grow in a hydroponic climate, but that doesn't mean it can't. It takes up to two weeks for celery seeds to germinate, which is relatively long compared to other vegetables. A quicker option is to use the celery stalk which you bought from the supermarket.

If you take the stalk from the bottom and cut it 2 inches, then place the base in a plate of water at room temperature, it will actually start to grow after just a week. Celery requires plenty of water and a deep water system will be the best system to choose from. In addition to germinating seeds, celery harvesting may take up to a total of 4 months after the seeds have been planted.

Celery likes a pH of 6.5, and the EC nutrient levels should be 1.8 to 2.4. There could be an accompanying plant in a growing room built for lettuce crops and cool weather crops. Temperatures in daytime will range between 58 and 80 degrees fahrenheit. Lighting is not intense and they need just about 6 hours a day.

Maturity and harvesting can take a long time and they can challenge a grower who needs patience but growing this crop can be one of the most rewarding given how costly it can be from the supermarket.

Benefits of Hydroponics to Grow Vegetables

The use of hydroponics to grow vegetables can be highly beneficial , especially in regions where conditions are not appropriate, or those times of the year when nothing is going to grow. Many of the above crops can be grown all year round, or you can grow these while planting any of the many others that aren't on the list in a different growing season.

No matter what you want to grow, there are countless benefits and here are a few you'll see:

Larger returns

Hydroponics can not make vegetables grow larger than their genetics allows them to grow, but they can grow to their full potential and in much less space than they can in the soil. The ability to control the levels of nutrients and pH in the water also ensures optimum growth for the vegetables leaving little room for failure.

Crops round the year

Since the gardener is in complete charge, as we have just seen, they can use artificial lighting and warning indoor growing conditions to grow through the year. Crops that are out of season are costly when brought in, so it makes all the difference to have them a few steps away from your kitchen!

Less Room

Hydroponic systems can be mounted almost anywhere. They may be hidden from any natural light indoors, or may be concealed in outdoor areas, or in a garden greenhouse. They can churn out many more crop harvests, but, with a much smaller area, that is possible than if the garden was in soil.

When a hydroponic garden is up and running, they can easily produce a large family with more than enough food.

Although some crops are unsuitable, there may be little need to buy some vegetables ever again. Many farmers start by only growing for consumption, but as they go along they find that they are increasing and need to start getting rid of vegetables because they produce so many.

Family and friends would be grateful for delicious fresh vegetables, but there are the shrewd farmers who are turning their gardens into small home businesses.

The above vegetables are just the tip of what hydroponics can bring. It's up to you to choose what you grow, but only the ones above mean you can choose from a wide variety. Start with these and as soon as you acquire more information, or find that you have that extra little room, you can broaden and tackle herbs, strawberries or anything else you think is hard to get where you live.

CHAPTER SEVEN

Herbs to Grow in Hydroponics

If you grow herbs for culinary or medicinal purposes it doesn't matter, hydroponics is a perfect way to grow them. There are several reasons to do so and the first is that they are rising faster. You can then add to this that they come with more flavor and aroma than counterparts grown in soil can. Research also shows that hydroponic herbs contain more aromatic oils up to 40 per cent.

Not only this, but growers can grow a variety of herbs that they would otherwise be struggling to grow in their own field.

Here are simple hydroponic herbs to grow:

- Basilika
- Kamele

- Romary

- Oregano

- Coriander

- Anise

- Dill Dill

- Catnip

Like all plants, the herbs are concerned with temperature, light and water. If you swing too low or too high for any of those herbs in either direction, they will end up dying. Growing herbs using hydroponics helps you keep yielding herbs whatever the weather or season. Hydroponic development takes up only less space and reduces water use.

Although all herbs can be simple to grow in a hydroponic system, here are the top eight herbs to grow. We're going to go over the fundamentals and benefits of each.

Basil

Basil is a common option for hydroponics since this herb is perfect to hold on to the aroma and flavor when used fresh. Those attributes are lacking on dried basil. So seeing restaurants and greenhouses using a hydroponics device for their basil herbs is not unusual.

All in all, there are 150 different basil species but the most common are:

- Delicious Basil
- Basil Genovese
- Sweet Basil Thai
- Purple Basil
- Basil Cemetery
- Basil Lime
- Basil Lettuce
- Piquant Basil

There are two ways you can plant basil, by germinating the seeds, or by planting cuttings which shape their roots within a week. Basil is a warm-weather herb, so keeping a temperature between 70-80 Fahrenheit is best. Blocks of rockwool are the most common media used in hydroponics with increasing basil. If you can use peat moss, coconut coir, perlite, and vermiculite, these may require sterilization prior to use.

Pythium is a threat to Basil seedlings, you should note. How exactly is Pythium? Pythium is a fungus which attacks many herbaceous crops and spreads disease. The best way to prevent pythium or other damping-off pathogens is to make sure your that media surface is not too humid.

When you get to harvest basil, the top 1/3 to 2/3's of the upper foliage can be cut. The plant will keep growing that back, so you can cut it again. Basil will regrow up to 2-3 times before removing the plant altogether and starting fresh is recommended.

Only cut the quantity of basil you need, this saves the worry of trying to keep it in good shape. Once you pick basil, basil's shelf life is only a few days, so it might be safer to keep it growing on the plant until it becomes essential. To see how easy it is to grow perpetual basil in a hydroponic system, you can check this video.

Chamomile

If you're a big tea fan, you might want to learn you can grow your own chamomile, indoors with hydroponics. Chamomile has many amazing antioxidant properties, which have been shown to reduce the risk of diseases such as heart disease and cancer. Often, they help combat insomnia and poor digestive problems.

Most would use a floating seed tray to help the chamomile seeds germinate. You'll want to get rid of the weakest ones after the seedlings grow to around 2 inches and there's just one solid seedling per cell in the tray. It can take up to 1-2 weeks for chamomile seed to germinate. Chamomile is recommended to receive up to 16 hours of light everyday.

Chamomile has wide versatility, as it applies to pH levels. It can range from 5.6 to 7.5 in anywhere. Ideally, you'll probably want to reach at 6.5 in the middle for optimal results to rise. You will be able to harvest your chamomile flowers after about 8 weeks.

The flowers can be picked by cutting off up to 3 inches of stem and then drying them in a sunny area on a rug. By not harvesting all the flowers you will make replanting much easier, which helps them to reseed themselves. For protection, store your chamomile in an airtight container in a dark, cool place.

Rosemary

This Mediterranean herb is an evergreen, with leaves that look like needles. The herb growing flowers in white, pink, purple, or sometimes blue. Rosemary may be used as an aid to a wide variety of issues, such as

- Digestion issues
- Stroke
- An appetite loss
- Cough
- Headaches
- Elevated blood pressure
- Blood pressure lowered
- Diabetes
- Repellent pest repellent
- And far more

Growing rosemary hydroponically can prove a lot slower compared to other herbs. You should predict a harvest time of up to 12 weeks, and the seed yields are often extremely low. They still prove much more efficient to grow hydroponically.

These herbs are susceptible to infections with the fungus, powdery mildew, and mites. The most suitable for this herb is an NFT hydroponic system and they should be subjected to temperatures ranging from 70 degrees Fahrenheit to 85 degrees Fahrenheit max.

Here are some fast tips to hydroponically grow the rosemary.

1. Maintain pH range from 5.5 to 7.0
2. Humidity rates will tend to be normal.
3. The herb should be exposed to at least 11 hours of daylight
4. You can harvest 2-3 times per sowing, and this can also be done during the year.

Oregano

Oregano is a member of the mint family and for thousands of years they used this herb for cooking and medicinal needs. Oregano was used by the ancient Greeks for treating GI illnesses, menstrual cramps, urinary tract infections, skin diseases, and dandruff. Many times they have studied oregano for its antimicrobial activity that wards off pathogenic Listeria.

Hydroponic Oregano should grow well in pH ranges from 6.0 to 9.0, and the level should fall between 6.0 and 8.0 for optimum performance. Rockwool cubes are commonly used to germinate the seeds that can take anywhere from 1 to 3 weeks. Some other common media are the Rapid Rooters, Oasis Root Cubes, or Grodan Stonewool.

Oregano is a slow grower, and after a transplant it can take up to 8 weeks before the first harvest. Oregano likes full sun when you grow outside, and when you grow under the lights the lighting won't be any different. T5 tubes are suitable for providing the right light, and they should be around 2 to 4 inches from the tops of the plant to prevent drying or burning the leaves.

Cilantro

From seed to harvest, when grown hydroponically, you are looking at about 50-55 days for cilantro. This choice of herb is very low maintenance, and needs no trimming. They can be harvested in part or in full.

If you're a food lover, you already know that which healthy cilantro is. Toppings, garnishes, salsas, this is what you call it. Although some people don't like the taste, why? A lot of people perceive the cilantro taste differently. Others describe it as a fresh and cool taste while others consider soap-like to their tastes. Here's a logical argument for that.

A few tips to develop hydroponic cilantro:

- Maintain a pH level of 6.5 to 6.7.

- Temperatures up to 75 degrees Fahrenheit will stay anywhere between 40 degrees Fahrenheit. Nevertheless, for temperatures in the 60s there are higher germination speeds.

- Watch out for spots of powdery mildew and bacterial leaves common to cilantro. These spots cause high humidity levels and exposure to too much humidity.

It does need plenty of water, but it doesn't have to be overwatered. Even it is recommended that oscillating air recreate a sturdier outdoor environment.

Anise

This uncommonly heard of herb has a taste of licorice. Often, it is also called aniseed. Although Anise can fight off many common problems such as digestion, gas, cramps, and more, other herbs also help.

Although the taste of the liquorice sort can leave it unpopular with many, it is resourceful in savoring bread, sausages, cookies, and cakes. Anise seedlings are very delicate and difficult to transfer, so it is best to allow the seeds to germinate and grow without moving them in their respective containers. You'll find the seeds can germinate for up to 2 weeks.

You're going to want to keep the pH range of about 5.5 to 6.5. Meeting at 6.0 in the middle is the most ideal for development. The seedlings get the most from having an oscillating fan stirring the wind gently for a few hours each day.

The best way to harvest anise is to cut the plant as required, and place it in a protected area free of direct sunlight to dry out. This can hang them upside down, too. They are harvested entirely as soon as the heads start appearing brown. Store away from heat and light, in an airtight jar. Anise usually has a shelf-life of up to 1 year.

Dill

Dill is an annual growing herb in the family of celery. It's most frequently seen grown in Eurasia where it is used to flavor milk. In your recipes you can use the fresh dill or dried dill. The stems aren't used when using fresh dill. Growing dill is very easy hydroponically, and thrives in this sort of growing climate.

Hydroponic Dill Growing Tips:

- Place and press the seeds on a piece of Rockwool. Keep the Rockwool moist with nutrients and water waiting for the seeds to germinate. Germination may take 7-10 days but can occur earlier.

- You may place the Rockwool directly into your hydroponic system after germination. Maintain pH range from 5.5 to 7.5.

- Allow enough space to grow, and note that the dill can often grow as high as three feet.

- Cut only the leafy leaves and discard the stems when the seeds tend to be brown and ripe.

Culinary dill applications include:

- Seals
- Salads
- Dips
- Pickles
- Casseroles

Uses for the medicine include:

- Relieving gas and stomach bloat
- Cramps
- Headaches

Catnip

If you have a cat, you may choose to grow this herb hydroponically mainly for their comfort and, of course, to provide yourself with some minor entertainment. Catnip is not only used for cats, somewhat contrary to common perceptions and the name itself. Catnip has been known since the early 1700s for its capacity to alleviate cramps and indigestion when used in herbal teas.

Here are some tips to cultivate the catnip indoors hydroponically:

- Catnip can be quickly propagated using cuttings or seeds with leaf tips.
- Have up to 5 hours of daylight.
- Ensure a reliable water supply with adequate drainage. Catnip can be susceptible to root rot so try avoiding an area that is too wet.
- Beware of the growth of molds, which can happen with too much misting.
- Eliminate any insect infestations, including aphids, mealybugs, scale, and whitefly;
- Don't let a cat get close to your system!

Is it Better to Grow Herbs Hydroponically?

Like often, when it comes to efficiently growing plants and crops, hydroponic systems emerge like top contenders do. Herbs will benefit the most from the ability of the watering system to receive a constant supply of nutrients and oxygen. In a hydroponic climate, on average herbs grow about 25 percent to 50 percent faster than an outdoor soil climate.

However, some herbs are better off being young. Hydroponic systems give their customers the ability to produce fresh herbs for restaurants, supermarkets, and commercial growers, which allows for greater flavor and cost-efficiency.

Consider certain benefits of hydroponically growing your herbs:

- They don't need any dirt. While some that love the naturist appeal of dirtying your hands by gardening out the sunlight, the truth is, some of us prefer not to have to go that direction. Hydroponic growth really requires only some water and clear mediums.
- You are going to get bigger yields and faster production. As previously stated, in a hydroponic system you will see 25 to 50 percent faster growth than you would as an outdoor crop. This faster growth means you'll be able to yield more in less time.

- Less maintenance. Most hydroponic systems are running on autopilot, so you can only test the pH balance and refill the nutrient solution regularly.

- Herbs most commonly fall prey to insects and pests. The possession of an indoor hydroponic system will significantly eliminate those threats.

- More water you'll conserve. On average, hydroponic systems only use up to 10 percent of the water used by outdoor soil plants. The water is filtered and continuously reused.

- The atmosphere is controllable. Is your area prone to floods, storms or even temperatures that are frigid? For an indoor hydroponic device, which will also be in a tightly regulated and secure environment, you don't have to think about this.

- You don't need to use herbicides or insecticides, meaning you can keep your herbs 100% organic and free from harmful chemicals.

- By using hydroponic gardening, you'll save considerable space. Systems can be customized, and even vertically installed.

- Some say hydroponic gardening helps with stress relief. There's always plenty to put within your home a part of your outdoor world. Having another living breathing element close you can have positive effects on mental health.

- It's an all-round fun hobby to get into, what's better than the satisfaction you get from knowing you've grown a plant from beginning to end, nurturing it every step of the way? Whether you have a natural green thumb or not, hydroponics is straightforward, for beginners too!

CHAPTER EIGHT

How To Clean A Hydroponic System: A Step-By-Step Guide

Every grower knows what keeping their hydroponic growing room clean and tidy means. Because we grow plants in sterile environments, any sign of bacteria or algae or pathogens can quickly ruin a plant crop in one matter our hours or a couple of days.

Although these growers keep their areas as clean as possible, the systems themselves need to be tendentious to be. Keeping clean is not enough at this point and a hydroponic system would require more than just sanitizing.

When you have finished one harvest and ready stuff for another, sterilization will make all the difference.

Here, we will examine how important it is to keep growing areas clean and what the difference is between sanitizing a system and thoroughly sterilizing one. With this we will look at the supplies you need, the cleaning agents you need, and how you need to use them effectively in a healthy way. We will be going through the entire cleaning process to finish.

We'll also look at some do and don't, and anything else that might be important to cleaning up your growing room.

Why Keeping Clean is Important

Although the health of your plants is vital, the one most significant justification for cleaning rising rooms is the health of all those who can use the bounty of a good harvest. Human health is the most important reason for doing these regular cleanings.

Many reasons for keeping clean and sterile are farmers who are already, or who are planning to have hydroponic systems for business projects.

Certifications and guidelines may be available and need to be followed.

Sanitization Vs. Sterilization: The Difference

There is often confusion between the two but in their approach and the end results, sanitizing and sterilizing a growing room and system are different.

Sanitization is the ongoing maintenance, and it's seen as keeping things clean and tidy in the most basic form.

Spilled water, dead plant matter, air intake filters are all part of this regular maintenance, and will affect the overall performance of your system.

All these three places are breeding grounds for bacteria and they can spread rapidly to your plants if not cleaned up.

When you look at a system's sterilization, it's more in-depth, because this includes cleaning up the physical system along with all the other components of your expanding region.

You will rid the entire growing area of viruses, bacteria, fungi, and microorganisms while performing sterilization.

You are preventing spread of any pathogens or forms of mildew in the times you sterilize your system.

Most of the time, after a harvest, sterilization is required.

If you have a separate growing area where your plants can be transferred when sterilizing, then this is perfect. That, however, is a luxury for many and not always possible.

The two differ, and growers should never think that sterilization alone is enough.

Between these periods the need for sanitization still exists.

Both are required, and different materials and processes must be employed.

Materials Required for Sanitization and Sterilization of Hydroponic Systems

If you intend to clean your house, you'll need some collection of tools and cleaning agents to get rid of your microorganisms house.

Tools Needed

- Pads of black scrub sponges

- Rigid spray brushes

- Tank brushes

- Long treated brush

- Mop and goosebump

- Gloves and rubber goggles

- Clippers and scissors – cut dead plant material that has not decayed

- Dry / wet vacuum

- Pick up rags

- Compressed air cans-perfect for cleaning ballast and control panel ventilation grills

- Seals to spare

- Garden fitted with female fitting adapter

CONCLUSION

The hydroponic system is not a soil-planting alternative. It's a great opportunity for those garden lovers who want a garden. This allows the gardener the correct sum and cost of using the land for the garden. The device is an ancient planting approach that was reinvented 100 years ago.

A properly built hydroponic system contains less water and fertilizer wastage than soil-based farms. Both water and nutrients are fed directly into the plants' root structure and recycled through the hydroponic system. It also reduces the usual possibilities of land and water contamination due to overland drainage and runoff, respectively.

All of this ensures the system requires less water and less supply of nutrients. Both of these aspects provide great economic benefits by reducing ongoing cultivation costs, thus paving the way for sustainable farming. This is critical in regions that are rated as having extreme water scarcity.

The likelihood of illness is largely reduced in the absence of the soil medium. That's a different plus factor. Traditional methods of cultivation are ground based. If soil-based farming is very different from hydroponic method the work intensity. Traditional agriculture involves soil tillage and cultivation. Until the actually rising season, all of these tasks are time consuming and labour-intensive. Other hydroponics considerations plus are the control of plant density and increasing climate humidity.